SOFAR

SOFAR

Poems

Elizabeth Bradfield

A Karen & Michael Braziller Book

PERSEA BOOKS

New York

Persea Books, Inc.
90 Broad Street
New York, New York 10004

LIBRARY OF CONGRESS CATALOGING-IN-PUBLICATION DATA
Names: Bradfield, Elizabeth, author.
Title: SOFAR : poems / Elizabeth Bradfield.
Description: New York : Persea Books, 2025. | "A Karen & Michael Braziller book" | Summary: "Taking its title from the acronym for the 'sound frequency and ranging channel,' a deep layer of oceanic water that enables sound to travel vast distances, Elizabeth Bradfield's sixth poetry collection draws on her knowledge of the sea (especially the waters and shoreline of Cape Cod), plumbing what can be heard by listening across the vast distances of our lives-and to strangers, beloveds, and the more-than-human world"—Provided by publisher.
Identifiers: LCCN 2025002435 (print) | LCCN 2025002436 (ebook) | ISBN 9780892556182 (paperback ; acid-free paper) | ISBN 9780892556199 (ebk)
Subjects: LCGFT: Poetry.
Classification: LCC PS3602.R3396 S64 2025 (print) | LCC PS3602.R3396 (ebook) | DDC 811/.6—dc23/eng/20250424
LC record available at https://lccn.loc.gov/2025002435
LC ebook record available at https://lccn.loc.gov/2025002436

Book design and composition by Rita Skingle
Typeset in Minion Pro
Manufactured in the United States of America. Printed on acid-free paper.

for the Sea Hags
in all your weathered, joyous, generous,
attentive, embodied beauty

CONTENTS

⌒

Considering the Hadal Zone / 3

List / 5

Erratic / 6

Sheath / 7

Shadow (*Carcharodon carcharias*) / 8

Tender: / 10

Cleat / 11

Origin Story, Re-wrought / 12

Silver Hake / 14

Lesson III: The Divisions, Illustrated / 16

Touchy / 18

The Paper Wasps / 20

Spinnaker / 21

Intergenerational / 23

〜〜

Marlinspike / 27

Articulation / 28

Drone / 29

General Questions / 31

A Mouth Like a Sailor / 32

Hawse / 33

Allegiance / 34

Devil's Claw / 35

Fulcrum / 36

Notes on the Wharf / 38

~~~

At the Smallpox Cemetery, Provincetown / 41

Remember the way / 43

The California Coast / 44

Hatch / 45

At fifty, I discover *vagility* / 46

Sissy-Fists / 47

Ded Reckoning / 48

Chock / 49

A Map, A Body Afloat / 50

From Sea, Toward Sea / 52

Learning to Swim / 54

Kept / 55

Plastic: A Personal History / 56

At the Mütter Museum / 58

~~~

Bell / 61

First Love / 62

Kiss me like a limpkin / 63

Skiff / 64

Outer Space or Deep Ocean / 65

Swaddled, No Matter / 66

Lesson VIII: Map of North America / 68

Imago / 69

Highland Light / 70

On Reality / 71

The Guides Go Ashore Ahead / 72

Taking a fix / 73

April, Provincetown / 74

Identification / 75

Building a Greenland Kayak / 77

In Lyme Country / 78

Permeable / 79

Today, Alongside a Fresh-dead Humpback Whale / 81

"Memory Rowing the Passage of Time" / 82

Appendix: To Draw a Map of the World / 83

Dispatch from this Summer / 84

Held/Treasured/Secret / 86

When One Known to You Dies,
the Rearranging of Space and Time Begins / 87

Binnacle / 89

Under the Great Wave / 90

All Without Incident / 92

Notes / 95

Acknowledgments / 98

The SOFAR (Sound Fixing and Ranging) channel exists in the ocean at a particular depth, pressure, and temperature and functions like a fiber-optic cable does for light, letting sound travel and travel and travel across distances otherwise impossible.

~~~~~

Think of the ocean as consisting of various zones, or layers—sort of like oil and vinegar salad dressing before it's shaken up—except that ocean layers occur due to differences in salinity (salt content) and temperature variations. . . . Because of SOFAR, sound emitted at a certain depth bounces between these various layers and can travel for hundreds of miles.
—NOAA (National Oceanic and Atmospheric Administration)

~~~~~

No one could write truthfully about the sea and leave out the poetry.
—Rachel Carson, The Sea Around Us

In every culture, the oldest memory is water.
—Robin Coste Lewis, To the Realization of Perfect Helplessness

A mythology of waters in its entirety would be simply history.
—Gaston Bachelard, Water and Dreams

⌢

I take the hydrophone, that silver bob,
marshmallow-sized, and lean
over the harbor, pay out

the black cord yard by fathom.
Tide and current vibrato it. I can't,
from here, drop far enough to reach

that perfect depth, that sound channel,
not in this water, or with this, but
I'll listen to what I can.

CONSIDERING THE HADAL ZONE

1.

Cusk eels in the harbor ratchet for love
all August. We hear them buzz
at night, desire sounded as thumb
up washboard, pulsed from where
we anchor.
                    The deepest
ocean trenches are named for Hades, god
of the underworld, who waits for love
to fall to him. In that dark, isopods
feed on what drifts down from sunlit
water: tissue, eelgrass, shipwood,
Fukishima's radionuclides.

2.

The sea floor is mapped by satellites
that ping the ocean surface and factor out
the waves that pass across it, leaving
swells and dimples pushed or pulled
by peaks and trenches deep below, proof
that what's hidden can still be sensed.

3.

                    There's a quartzite block
a half-fathom high and larger than a kingsize
bed to the east of Provincetown's Town Hall.
Its surface ripples with small waves stilled

forever, memorial to the disease that flooded
this town in the 80s, stormed those who held and cared
for all who fell to them from places that would not
hold care. I like to imagine, inside the block,

delicate, sensitive forms drifting and brushing
each other like cilia, sargassum,
or tentacles.

4.
            As a kid, my dream
was to live on the sea floor in a domed house
of glass. Last summer, on the Labrador ferry
coming in to Natuashish, we passed the ship
that weeks before had launched the sub
that sank to visit the *Titanic* and never
came back. On the ferry deck, a buzz

everywhere at once and hard to locate
like sound underwater to human ears
there are kids on deck I'd quit for sure is that
the crew in lawn chairs is that really they
must be so where are they going can
you imagine I hear the family how
long do you think they waited

5.

I wear both our wedding rings and your father's,
too, on my right ring finger. They click
quietly. Some cusk eels thrive in the Hadal
Zone's dark crush. The articles don't say
if they make any sound.

LIST

from Old Norse, border, selvage; earlier, spelled lust

To list is to edge
toward tipping, which sailors

know one way and the urban
dictionary another. I found you

alongside my desire for another. At
the edge of what felt right. And now,

here we are, almost thirty years
on, leaning from so much,

holding our edges.

I remember visiting the fabric
store with my mother, the bright

slide of scissors, clean rip of measured
cloth, and the magic of selvage,

a tidy, stippled border we knew wouldn't
fray, an advantage

in what we wanted to stitch
together. List. Lust. Lean

and listen. Please.

ERRATIC

glacially deposited rock differing from the size and type of rock native to the area in which it rests. From the Latin errare *(to wander)*

I come upon them sometimes
like today beside a favorite trail
in a month without leaves and before
snow which is to say now an unpredictable
time in a time when I too am unpredictable but
there it hunkers gray and strange in this land ground
into being by glaciers and deposited at their now-gone
feet I know something of where it came from
and how it got here but even though this is a daily
walk I'd not noticed it before and probably
wouldn't have noticed it until now
when my own body is in retreat
from its decades
of advance
        the change
it's called and it's as unexpected
as a boulder in an easy trail which your
strolling self must swerve around or
clamber over as you puzzle as you hitch
your pace for it is hard and inscrutable
mysterious in its looming strangeness
(why here? why the trail here, around it?)
strange and insurmountable as my adolescent
surging self was to myself then as this new
self is to me now surging and in retreat
this self which feels like a remnant
of that great transformation
and seems just as capable
of damage as any
ungiving thing

SHEATH

Cover for the blade
I'd earn my place by and trust
to fix and free what needs it. Dress

I slip my body in and out of and what
the coyote's penis slips from, too. This
morning, in February's raw, bright chop,

two on the beach, heads
down, sniffing something that doesn't
really matter. What matters is what they

smell in each other. His chin set on the dip
of her spine. Her tail lifted to one
side—after, calm.

Broad daylight on a beach that, come
summer, will be bright with towels
and bodies rank with sunscreen. Now

this harbor is empty, flecked with seasonal
moorings. Only us, now. Only those of us
lucky enough to have seen what winter

tries to tell us about the necessary dangers
and possibilities in being exposed.

Shadow (Carcharodon carcharias)

"The top predators in the oceans—great white sharks and some of their
kin—have an extra sense to help them find and track prey: the ability to
detect the tiny electrical fields that are generated by all living organisms . . .
They're so sensitive that they can even detect a beating heart."
  —Damond Benningfield, "Ampullae of Lorenzini"
   at www.scienceandthesea.org

For you, shadow, the skin-holding sea flickers,
surges with light, scent, the pulsed charges of
bird-heart, cod-heart, seal-heart.

> I have envied and feared those for whom the spirit veil
> is thin, who sense what to me is wind but
> for them is presence beyond birds.

Your eye, I learn, shadow, is able to see in both darkness and day,
is not black but indigo, a dye that harmed many more
in its enslaved making than your hungers ever have.

> Only twice have I been certain some spirit
> hovered near me. Once, the night I was married,
> on a sleeping porch beside the bay where I still swim.

You hover in the trough at slack tide, in the shadow
between sand bars, listening, listening with your other
senses, your body a tuning fork thrummed by other bodies.

> We woke in the night in that borrowed house
> on the bed in the winterized porch, something
> unhappy on the other side of the wall. Something. . . .

The quiet of you. How, the one time I saw you
from the cliff's ragged field site, you emerged
more than rose into sight, shadow, becoming presence.

A sound, a chair scraped. Thrum of ire. I held
my love and, instinctive, hardened into a shield, every
part of me *no*. And it faded. We could not return to dream.

I've seen what you've missed more than witnessed the taking:
punched curve at the hip of a seal, fresh pink-white or
furred-over scar. I've seen you slide up a dead whale's flank.

The friend whose house it was, unsurprised, told us
her mother had died there, her last years full of confused
pain. What did her spirit speak or seek?

I read that your body, unlike the bodies of whales, of turtles,
of tuna, lucky shadow, is not hurt by the poisons
(PCBs, mercury) we've sloughed into your ocean.

I felt myself shift into pity, then. Fear and fury
ebbed. With the senses I have, I can't sense much
of the worlds I live alongside, signaling over me.

Shadow, the tags that sound out your passage are nothing
but moments of presence, nothing of what pulls
you or what changes the skin you can shade at will.

Shadow, I don't seek or fear you but I know you're there,
under the bay's bright scrim, your senses vaster
and older than anything this body or the gray folds
of my human mind, fired by strange sparks, can know.

TENDER:

the little boat that gets
you from ship to shore,

a shuttle between
what bigger thing's carrying us
further or what land's

welcoming us back. What
can I tend? Attendant, I offer

not money (coin for care)
but notice, regard. Tension
of gaze, unwavering. In

tenderness we did register
ourselves with the state. And

the paper that binds us is
legal tender: now someone will pay
one of us the other's government share

after one of us dies. *Tendre,*
the origin, means extend,

stretch, proceed. I am
inclined to you and
tend you, toward you,

still, even as we drift . . .
o little, rowable boat

CLEAT

The first time I held a wrist-fat multistrand line
and flopped it down (cross tuck cross)
over a shin-long cleat

the sense of motion, pattern, right-doing
was almost sexual—as different

from the thumb-thick rope
I'd used until then as a parent's
sweet peck is from a lover's mouth.

Origin Story, Re-wrought

For decades, I was part of a machine I loved.
She mothered me, raised me up from what sad self
I was, bookish, theoretical, unbodied. By

dog watch. By heaving line, by windlass
and engine rounds, by *Roger that*
I learned a life. She was conservative,

this mother. Her corporate
particulars: *guest* not passenger, *stateroom*
not cabin. No visible tattoos allowed back then. No

piercings other than the two small lobe-holes girls
were permitted. She pretended to not notice
my nose ring, my raised eyebrow. I loved

the stories she told at night, in the darkened
pilot house, as I watched with captain or mate
for real dangers (we once ran aground) and the predicted

navigational winks telling us where we were (where?)
and what to avoid. What to avoid? Whistling, bananas,
women, queers. My first true love and I chuckled

and kissed in the gear locker, breast
to breast. Look. I slept inside her (that mother).
I slept inside her with my siblings: Frank and Nori

and Tom and Michael. Or, more exactly, we shared
cabins, bunk by bunk, watch by watch. We slept
together in the spell of what it was

to choose to sleep there. And the older,
cooler cousins (officers, engineers, naturalists
who'd lived this for decades)—I studied them.

Sometimes I, too, pulled up the long brass zipper
of my boiler suit and got ready to grind metal or paint
a rail with toxic stuff that would endure a while in the tough

air. Sometimes I, too, drove the Zodiac, stood
with hand on tiller, left knee braced against the port
pontoon, seeking bird, sea lion. Years later, my youth purged,

they welcomed me. Let me lecture on bears or whales or
lichen. Sometimes I—ahh, fuck it. Listen. We were fooling
ourselves, even then. Even then, in those days, we knew
there was rot and wrong in this. Or we should have.

SILVER HAKE

Thrash splash at the edge
of vision. Fish at the marsh
edge on an ebb tide. I walked
over. Took a photo. A photo. A
photo. In air, gold-eyed
and rust speckled. How long

that moment for the fish,
for me. Then I put my hands
just behind the gills, breathed
into right grip & moved
so water could pass over frill.
I called up to ask if anyone

would like to see? To see? They
shook their heads, silent, silhouetted
against sky. They knew better
than me. And so I let it—
silver hake—go. I thought
I'd seen it so clearly, slick, vivid

muscle in my hands, bronze
body in bronze sand. But,
home, I flipped through, pinched
and zoomed, held & beheld
again, which is when

I saw the perfect circle pressed
into flank which had to be made
by one ring of a scalloper's mesh bag.
Which is why—bycaught & unwanted,
disallowed & so tossed back

as the crew steamed home, shucking
& tossing all but the marketable

muscle, marsh sucking tide into
its big lungs—we came upon this fish
who shares a blush

with the scallop's shell. Who
swims over their beds. Who wasn't
intended to be caught up in all this
but was.

LESSON III: THE DIVISIONS, ILLUSTRATED

redacted from Smith's Quarto, or Second Book in Geography, *1848*

What are Oceans?   Ocean? (see the corners of
the Maps.) What ocean separates   ? America
from Africa? America from Asia?

            Name the oceans?

A SEA is a large body. The whole body
        sometimes.

                Africa from Europe?
Africa from Asia?   southeast of Asia?   East of
        What sea?   Ocean?   Which?

                sea, interspersed

A GULF   a body
        extending.

What gulf   ?
                What?

A STRAIT is a narrow body.
                America? separate   connect
        straits   What, between?
What do they connect?

                connected and   separated   each

A LAKE is a body.   The water &c., is
        The water.
How long?

water flowing
into an   other body.

Into what does it flow?   Into what does it
flow?

                Into what do they unitedly flow?
        Into what do they flow?
     Africa, into what does it flow?
Asia, and into what do they flow?
     natural divisions?

Name the Grand Divisions.
     largest   ?   Largest ?
Largest?   Largest   ? Largest gulf?

Touchy

we say, when someone's
sensitive. So touchy. So
dangerous & delicate &
ready to tip. *Touching*,
though, is sweet. And we
are *touched* by the gift,
the thought. Moved
into knowledge of care
if not love. Touched, too,
means crazy. God-kissed.
The brain lit otherwise. I hope
we've all known someone
who has *got the touch,* able
to ease a knot, make any machine
hum true, tune a string. And
Touch me, says Stanley, in
the poem that always
chokes me up. As if the hand
of a wife would bring me back
to myself or to the selves
we both once were. *Don't
touch*: first warning.
The stove, the open socket's
shock, the body unknown
to you & all the bodies
it, in turn, has, willfully
or not, allowed such
intimacy. When I first
felt yearning for the skin
I always kept hidden
to touch another's
hidden skin, it was
the early decade of a different
terrible virus. The danger
was known & unknown

both. And, in some small
way, the risk of infection
not unlike the risk
of intimacy. *In touch*, when
we know how someone
is faring. *Touch-and-go*,
when we're not sure
how things will turn out.

THE PAPER WASPS

In each of the fourteen jars on the sill
above my desk: a paper wasp. I didn't know

what else to do when they started bumbling
the room's air, long legs dangling like an airlifted cow's.

I watch them clean their beautiful faces. I watch them
move up and down the jarsides. They can see

each other, and me, warbled through the lettering. I put
myself in this room most days, put my mind into

the machine before me. At first I'd usher them out,
open the door to spring's thin air. But more and more

kept coming and I wanted to forget my body.
Only one so far has died, dry and curled. I could

put it outside for the birds. I could use the jar
for another and another and I don't think

I'd feel badly if I didn't put them on the shelf above
the screen of the thing I put myself into. But

I did. So I watch them, accountable to and
compelled by them, by my own calm

cruelty. Of course, I could release
us. Of course I could do that.

Spinnaker

Spinnaker, eleven when she died after suffering four separate
entanglements, is a humpback whale whose rearticulated skeleton
is preserved at the Center for Coastal Studies in Provincetown.
She is the only such whale displayed with her entangling material
still intact and visible.

The bones' oil still seeping even though she's hung
here almost a decade, unmoving. Dust gathers
on her skull, her scapulae. One member of the team

who cut her free of nets and ropes three times climbs
a ladder with a feather duster to remove what she'd
not have felt in life. Broken vomer, broken

orbital socket. Mouth stripped of baleen to share
and show and study, a decade's worth of surge and
ebb: cortisol, progesterone, trophic levels in those fibers.

Her flukes are a plaster replica of what can't be preserved.
The oil that browns her bleached bones, that leaches
from their pores and stains the white they weren't

in her body, the white they were when she first
was trucked back from where she'd beached then been
buried and beetled-cleaned. I stood on a ladder, helped

sponge-pat pattern into clay between her vertebrae
meant to mimic softer tissue. Now I'm under her ribs
with a group of poets. One student asks

if we ever have funerals for the whales. She lives
in a country that holds services for glaciers. Not
every vertebra is stained, which is evidence not

of good work by the cleaners but of Spinnaker's hunger,
the absence of stored fat in her hurt body. Last week, I watched
Spinnaker's mother, Palette, loll on her back and slap

her great pectorals down. In play. In joy. I'm fairly sure
she doesn't know she's lost a daughter or that we've displayed her,
killing net and rope still embedded in her skull.

I've read of a right whale who nursed another's
calf and abandoned her own—careless or generous
swap, we don't know. Without the rope or the seep

of oil I think I'd feel less tenderness for Spinnaker's
great, pre-teen body. She'd be more object, less
interrupted living self. Priests touch oil to the brows

of supplicants as they look up. I look up. Nothing falls.

INTERGENERATIONAL

A mother pulls from all she's taken up—
herring, pesticides, salmon, pharmaceuticals.

Decades she's put it where it'll keep, in
fat, layered around heart, teat, gut—a comfort-

er against the ocean's chill, the future's lack.
Then she passes the world she's swum to her young.

An orca in the Salish Sea or
beluga in the St. Lawrence, washed ashore,

is hazardous, is sent somewhere
safe from scavengers, from leach.

A son has no choice, must
nurse and keep it all. A daughter?

She's luckier. She might get the chance
to start fresh when her own kids pull it down.

~

Imagine the bob, passive as an angler fish's
dangle, ready to capture sound. I crane
to translate what pings and thrums

up-wire, pushing now against my ear's drum:
hull-slap, prop-whine. The beloved frustration
of white noise, spun time which resolves

into sea robin, cusk-eel, white-sided
dolphin—what am I, human
and other, even listening for?

MARLINSPIKE

One of my knives has one, smooth
curve fitted to the folded blade. Like
a stem or claw. I think of it

as one of my tusks. Sailors are always
checking out each other's knives.
You want at least two:

one to thumb-flip open and quick-
cut you free, one to work the problem
with driver heads and pliers.

Phone, wallet, keys, knife, the hand
checks its stations. I've got a drawer
of knives including the red Swiss Army

my grandfather gave me as a girl,
despite the fact I was a girl. Oh, the
snick/click as tweezers or toothpick

slide home. When a Coastie showed me
his special knife etched with a bowhead
I didn't tell him I have one just like it.

I open the spike, imagine shoving it
into three-strand, making a way
to splice an eye or open a knot

so I can drift at last
from what holds us tight, what
binds us to such boring normalcy.

Articulation

My first winter in Provincetown revealed a humpback's
spine in the marsh. I assumed such wonders
always showed up here, then

twenty years went by before I'd see
a ghost whale laid out on an easy beach.
But lately? Humpback, humpback,

finner again and again washed up.
Last spring and summer, I watched one
scatter. Ribs in with driftwood,

jaw-glow under my kayak. Someone propped up
the skull, chin to sky. Wonder and attention
were stitched into sand by gulls, people, dogs, but

I also saw the angularity
of saw in bone and a hole drilled
to thread a line and haul away

this skull, this whale,
who swam along and beyond us, who
we watched feed and nap and dive. Someone

bent over the body with force and desire. Look.
I've done it. I have blocked out
the living being and all she carried

and tasted and can carry and taste
for others in death. I've taken, collected.
Made body an object. Wanted and violated.

DRONE

Over reindeer. Over
swimming walrus glacial
outwash cleft of nesting
kittiwakes, their own wild swirl
sounding up, harsh
and louder.
                    Over us
walking tundra or a river's silt
murmur (we look up,
diverted).
                    If I had a slingshot,
if my rifle were sanctioned
for this.
                    Over moss campion over iceberg
sweating on the beach.
                                        Small
solace only one's sanctioned
per ship, per trip. *Eye of the voyage*
every videographer says
they need. To sell what
they shoot, unique.
                                        Need
need.
            Whine of a word
                    above us,
        interrupting.

                    One trip, by
permission of the captain who
gets to say yet doesn't know or
can't see harm, flown to hover over
a polar bear.
                    Ambling bear, continuous
            bear, bear who craned

to look, who, pulse up, sped
getting hotter and didn't couldn't swat,
didn't couldn't stop, sit, scratch
behind a tiny,
white ear.
The captain said the bear
would walk anyway
so *why not.*

GENERAL QUESTIONS

redacted from Smith's Quarto, or Second Book in Geography, *1848*

What are the natural divisions   ?

What is a   Gulf   ?

What are parallels   What is a degree
            How is it reckoned?

How is the human family divided?
What is religion, and how divided?
What are the general divisions of North America?

What gulfs   separate   When
and by whom   For what

Will you bound your own   import   ?

*Note: It would be well for the teacher to continue the questions
on the learner's own state.*

What privileges has each   ?
      For how long, and by whom are they chosen?

      What   For what   In what
                  Which is appropriated ?

      Which is the largest division?
                  For what is it celebrated?

A Mouth Like a Sailor

You hawse-dog. You chock

block & scupper plug. Bollard.

You're a pintle in my gudgeon.

Davit swinger. Your binnacle's

deviant & your hatch is not

tight. Into the laz, lubber line.

You're a hard chine. Wrong-

reeved. A knot's in your bight

& your hawser won't haul. Skivvy

waver. You're afterbrow

& your thruster's got

no dig. Stick a fid in your splice.

You wouldn't know fancywork

if it hit you with a French

whip. Deadeye. Seacock.

Limber hole. Kedge it

& the capstan you came in on.

You'll never come about. You'll

never make way with me. I'm not

your waypoint, not

your following sea.

HAWSE

O opening to sea, passing through
yourself what holds us: chain,
cable, anchor.

The whole bow shuddered
when we let the drum
spool out and links staccatoed

your tube. *Come up
the hawse* a term for when
anyone makes their way

from deckhand to bridge
officer by apprenticeship not
classrooms or certificates.

I was white, had
teeth, could look an officer
who'd take a chance

on me in the eye with
the mix of pride and chosen
debasement that worked

for them: tough yet pliable,
able to squeeze into a shape
that let me hook

to what I longed
to fix myself to
for a long while.

ALLEGIANCE

Each morning before light, in
season, Billy's F-150 fires
up, grumbles in his drive,
heads for the pier. I hear it
through the small window above
my bed, and when I'm out,
I watch for him—Billy at the Race,
Billy off the Peaked Hill, Billy steaming
home around the point. Billy. Thick
glasses, accent, hands, wizard
of fiberglass and steam box, torch
and epoxy, whose loft holds all
the tools, any clamp or nail you'd
need, any saw or grinder. Who
coaches us as we fix our skiff in his
garage and doesn't laugh
in a mean way when we
fuck up. *How's my favorite*
whale hugger? calls Billy
as I drive my Prius past his house.
We call him *The Boat Fairy.* To his face.
He and his wife call us *The Girls.* We
avoid politics beyond weather
and fish, which we get into
big time, elbows out windows,
idling. We want to make him
a T-shirt, a badge, a sticker
for his truck. We tell him so. Listen:
we all know there are silences
between us. It's ok to not
speak them here.

DEVIL'S CLAW

Have you held the devil's
claw? Curled your fingers
over its curl and hooked
the chain safe? Have you

released it? Let the claw clang
loose then eased
the drum's break, dropped chain
and anchor down and down,

leaned over the bow to see
if the anchor took, then set the dog
and walked away? Have you
slept on the hook? Did you drag?

I have. I have. And now I wonder what
all that trust did to me. For sure,
it saved me. Though that's
troubled, metaphorically.

The devil's claw is backup
if you haven't turned the brake tight. If
some rogue wave knocks the dog out.
It's the devil's claw we trust, two

curves hooked over a chain's link
looking up at whoever's at
the helm, seeing if we know
how close to danger we've always been.

Fulcrum

It was summer and winter at once
in the harbor's west end, season teetering,

skipping, it seems, spring altogether. Sixty gray seals
rested where, all season, they'll rest and moan

near the dropoff's swift gradation toward dark.

Early light. Recent fog. Beneath us, horseshoe crabs
in pairs clasped and shoveling into sand. Scoters,

bright-billed and late this cold May to depart.
Black bellied plovers staging on shore before

heading north. Then the morning's surprise—a storm

petrel at rest on the water. We fell into our usual
chatter, you saying *Not so strange.* Me

sure it's the *first time ever* to see this bird we mostly
catch fluttering, fluttering above waves, delicate

webbed feet trailing. We put the sun

behind us, pulled out the camera. *Probably
sick,* we said when it didn't take flight. But what if

this gift has no sorrow wrapping it? What then do we know

of the world? I've been faithful to you for nearly thirty
years and now my body's becoming a new weather.

It was winter and summer at once. We are old
and strange to each other within the shelter

of a place still recognizable on maps centuries old,
a place that shifts with each storm, each tide.

Notes on the Wharf

Winters, I come to check for birds. Gust-bumped, binos up: snowy owl, guillemot, dovekie, bufflehead, loon. Could it be a king eider year?

Certain summer nights we find it all—life ring stations, bulkheads, harbormaster's office, trash barrels—black-spattered with squid ink. Jerked up with lures, lured by light, skin defiant of singularity. Townies and out-of-towners shoulder to uneasy shoulder.

Trucks, rust-buckets and new-leased, hunker parked by the dingy dock. *Commercial fishers only.*

On Cabral's gorgeous wreckage of a building: huge portraits of women (Almeda, Eva, Mary, Bea. Frances gone to weather but a frame still holding her space.) stand in and look out for all the women of this sea-facing shore who for centuries have watched us leave and return. Leave and return. Always the welcome furrows of their watchfulness.

Ship whistles sound up through town and signal departures: one long and three short. My summer clocking, even ashore.

Love, you bicycled to my boat when DOMA was struck down. All the town's bells, church and government, were pealing across the water. From the pier, over the stretch of lines that moored me, your glad shout: "I guess we're getting married!"

Each time I go, I check for the boats I know. *Raider, Crash, Lisa Zee, Rhumb Line, Bay Lady, Ginny G, Cee Jay, Ibis.*

Absences are their own memorials. I visit them here, too.

~~~

One night we anchored out, wavelets
loud on the hull, and sound woke us.
I fumbled gear, dropped the bob. What

omygod omygod what? buzzed upwire and also
in air? A drilling that came to sound like gnashing,
loud and angry and strange. I could be wrong. Maybe

it was feasting glee, party chatter, love song lullaby
duende for an other mind. It didn't stop so we tried
again to sleep, stars continuing their slow spin,

AT THE SMALLPOX CEMETERY, PROVINCETOWN

after CD Wright's Casting Deep Shade

"Beech is Anglo-Saxon *boc*: book, document, or
charter," CD writes. "The shoots grow faster
in the dark," she writes in her 250-some page chronicle
of obsession. Here, now, at the smallpox cemetery
near where I live, the shin-high marble grave markers,
corners softened, stand canted, like awkward lumber.
Bone-white, chiseled only *No. 1, 2, 14*, they are
shaded under this grove of not-yet-dying American
beech. Dogs bark in the distance. In the 1800s, the fevered
were brought to this Pest House, to bunks far
from town, by men who needed the extra scratch
bad. They'd not have heard dogs. All pets were killed
by town decree. One of the graves holds Antone
Domingo, 22, who stepped off a ship from the Azores
already a widower. Some local desperate for cash
would have buried him and Mary Rogers, who came
from Boston by steamer then died in just six days.
There's still canopy over the road that leads here, but
many leaves are striped dark, have clawed into themselves,
a sure sign the tree will soon be dead. No treatment for this
outbreak, which is *natural*, which doesn't mean it isn't awful.
Can you imagine this world without beech trees? Also
dead in 1872: George Hallett, Frank Sofrine, Manuel
Terciera, Tasmin Manuel, whose husband gave it to her then
listed her as *heart attack* so she could be buried proper
in another, less lonely place. "Use a beech branch as a wand
to open channels for communication with spirits," she writes.
She writes, "caterpillars that eat beech leaves include the ghost
moth." The doctor paid to tend the sick could not return
to visit home. Another doctor, to prove it safe, shot
vaccine into his five-year-old. A few of the markers
are broken or gone. All winter, the leaves, marcescent,

shiver in the slightest wind, pale tan and thin as onionskin.
They preserve the shape of summer's light-eating tree that,
with luck, will hunger for summers to come. Mask
in pocket, hands in pockets, I stand by inkberry and bull
briar above the small hole that marks the pestilence
house's cellar. Above, beautiful, green, another mourning.

REMEMBER THE WAY

we'd clean ourselves
for each other? The baths,
ritualized or hasty, whole
or part. And then the sweet
funk of your body rising
through the soaps,
the mildly scented
lotions. Rising
from joints and crooks:
armpit, neck, crotch.
How annoyed I was
sometimes at that pause
between desire's spark
and its warm flesh.
How cold the house
in winter, when we'd
bundle rather than
dial up the thermostat's
expensive face. We saved
that extra for hot
water. For sweet oils
we'd buy and use
to rub each other's
bared skin smooth.

THE CALIFORNIA COAST

Offshore, the sea lions wouldn't stop
barking. I didn't want them to. Not
ever—through the thin tent walls: sea lions.
Over surf, under pines, along the high
chittering of oystercatchers. Inland,

fires were burning. We didn't live here,
so didn't know how wrong the noon sky,
the sunset, the gorgeous, flushed dawn. We
loved it. We wanted to move here. Back home,
the bay froze, sea turtles were stopped mid-

paddle. But we were off the grid, nearly
barefoot, basking. We shat in a hole. We tossed
our rinsewater out the trailer's door. It was truly
paradise at the pink camper until I suggested we go
walk in the redwoods. Off the coast, off

the conservation land, we found etched
into dirt and cobbled river bed what's
found everywhere. Rage. A doorless white truck,
forever stalled, rusting, and left. *Fuck it.*
On one oxbow shore: blue panties with lace trim,

straw-brimmed hat on a stump, dusty
sweatshirt—a story we didn't want
to imagine. Boredom and the violence
of being bored. Back home it's told
differently, sculpted with other debris,

hidden under other veneers. But,
America, it's everywhere.

HATCH

is open! we shout, voices echoing
the cabin when we pull up the D-ring
set into the deck and hoist

the hinged square. There's
a hole in the middle
of the floor now. *Hatch*

is open! With drama, with
verve. Someone could fall in. Someone
could break something at the base

of the ladder among the boxes
of candy, napkins, and beer. Someone
climbs down, gathers what's needed

and hands it up to someone who stands over
to grab what's held up. Hatch. Hold, void,
locker—(the private dark down there and how

it could be used). What we keep tucked
away, safe for when we need it.
A closed danger we walk across all day.

At fifty, I discover *vagility*

and I can't stop staring at it, saying
it. Vagility. Vagility. How can it not
mean estrogen-related volatility? The uterus

wandering, hysterical? Or a frail, keening
thrum of need unanswered, unanswerable.
Desire rejected like a wilted gladiola.

(I don't really know what a gladiola
looks like, but it sounds like there's a labia
in there somewhere. I'll look it up.) It only

means *the ability of an organism to move
about freely.* I am the vagile daughter,
dispersed from home shores.

I sought love. Found it. And got stuck
elsewhere. *Vagus* means wandering. My days vaguer
and vaguer. Was it yesterday or last year

that I saw you, that I was seen? Where
did the time go? What happens to the body
when the surges that paced it suddenly go slack?

Have you ever thought of it that way? Why
not? Wait. Where are you going now?

Sissy-Fists

was my favorite costume of that year's Carnival
parade. Pink sateen shorts, pink boxing
gloves, papier-mâché rock mounded
in a small shopping cart. I could never

be that witty about my burdens,

not even if I tried real hard. He was gray,
wiry. Spine curved like he'd been taking
a nap draped over a boulder. Sisyphus
is such a dumb myth. The rock. The

hill. Pushing. Repeat.

Why didn't he just walk away? There must
have been something serious at stake.
In the parade, his laurel was of lamb's ears,
his sash fixed by a gold brooch. Afterwards,

we had one of our familiar arguments,

and again I knew I wouldn't be the one
to leave. I like the rough of granite. It keeps
my palms nice and smooth. I like the way
my triceps look now, after all these years.

DED RECKONING

The sea's off somewhere, doing nothing. Listen.
            —*Elizabeth Bishop*

To know where you are and when
you'll get where you're going,

to *deduce* via *reckoning*, look to landmarks,
nav marks, winds, currents. The known

knowns. Which hold unknowns. Keep good
notes of what you pass, and when, what

direction you were headed at the time.
As a kid, I loved mysteries

that planted clues then showed you
in the end what you had missed.

I honed my skills with cookie sheets
of objects *(what's gone?)* and secret

passwords *(what's the first present
I ever gave you?).*

Now, there is so much looking away.
And some of that is love. I still know

roughly where I am.

Chock

What the line passes through to reach
bollard or cleat bolted to dock
or deck
       a planned gap in the hull's flank,
wings to guide what secures us, rounded edges
to gentle the fray borne of storm surge or
passing wake.
            New weather has,
these years, shifted how we secure,
sweetheart, our boat.
             And I've tried
new configurations of spring,
breast, bow, and stern to buffer
any wear that would part
what holds us.

Listen:
       casting off, when I'm bent
to haul aboard a mooring line, eye
lifted free, bitter end lost

under what I've pulled and piled on deck,
all I can see through that small view
       is a little bit of pier

  then a darkening as we head out
into deeper water, the chock's
inner rim polished by all
we've pulled through it,
a frame shined
by years of use.

A Map, A Body Afloat

aloft it's   very bright.
    dangerously so.

and this is the
        light   bouncing

        and this is a body afloat

this is the surface   in both air and water &

of the water

---

all with their respective dangers

        this
     is a school   of fish
       shadowing
     beneath that scrim

and this is all I can't see even
if the water's clear   too
deep too deep
for light

and these are all the beings
you know are moving around. but not really. and

there are either more or less than you
can imagine

and here it's very dark
though some things glint
when disturbed

FROM SEA, TOWARD SEA

for Rachel Carson, for the American eel

Slippery selves, our origins. Out there,
      new, at sea, we mingle, borderless. Hatch
            from round worlds into currents

wafting sargassum's canopy. Undifferentiated
      by sex, adrift and hungry, slight enough
            to be picked up by anything—

eddy (sister), porbeagle (bully), loggerhead (mother)—
      and moved, no matter our will. Not
            even elvers yet. Just willow leaves tossing

in wind too big to sense as anything other than *home.*
      Then, months of becoming. Then, tasting tongues
            of sweet water, finding thirst, picking one. We don't

need to know why. What I know: I needed another home
      than my born-to to become myself, so I followed
            what felt right. In mixed salt, in brine, half-

home, half away, we writhed. I am sorry
      for those who found us, who reckoned with
            that naked and vulnerable joy. Then

we let ourselves run. Upriver. Hundreds of miles against
      what we'd never, until now, felt. Becoming
            she, he, they, me. The mixed estuary of *maybe*

not enough. Up through runnels, over dams and, rain-
      slick nights, even across fields no one imagined we
            could survive, until the right water

held us. The right, soft silt. We burrowed in, warm
in dark, warm through cold seasons, safe
from summer's piercing shine. Years.

Decades. Comfortable
enough despite the dangers of others' hungers.
Slick and twisting in anyone's hands who tried

to move us, slick in our own selves, twined.
I was satisfied. I grew. I won't tell you
what I learned of desire, loss, season, or

want. You know that for yourself.
And now. But now, despite me, it's time.
My eyes shift toward a different seeing,

grow larger and eager for dim, deep ocean light.
My body hungers for water that doesn't
hold me snug in banks but lets me

loose, again wildly alive and unnoticed or too small
for notice or away from the shores (at last) of
notice. I am no salmon, after all, no stickleback.

Ocean is origin and end.
Start and finish of my least known
days, where my body comes from,

where it goes. I go.

LEARNING TO SWIM

after Bob Hicok & Aracelis Girmay

Now forty-five, having outlasted some of
myself, I must reflect: what if I hadn't been held
by my mom in the YWCA basement
pool, her white hands slick under

my almost-toddler armpits, her thumbs
and fingers firm around my ribs (which
is to say my lungs), held gently as a liverwurst
sandwich and pulled, kindly, under?

What if I hadn't been taught to trust
water might safely erase me those years
I longed to erase or at least abandon care of
my disoriented, disdained body? I might have

drowned instead of just ebbed, never slid
from given embankments into this other
natural course.
                Drift and abundance in what
she offered. The wider, indifferent ocean
of trade and dark passage not yet

mine to reckon. And so now, sharp tang
of other waters known, I am afloat, skin-
chilled, core-warm, aware of what lurks
and grateful to trust and delight
in our improbable buoyancy.

—2019

KEPT

For over twenty years I saved the expensive
pink plastic & wire retainer that, after
my braces came off, I was instructed

to wear at night. Decades beside
my bed or loose on the shelf
in the bathroom. Every

few months, I'd put it in. See if
I'd slipped. Roof of my mouth
smooth & stifled. Why

did I keep it? Guilt each time
I put it in. Shame at the girl-thing
beside my adult bed. It disgusted

me. It pleased me when it fit. As if
that proved me good, still aligned
to the better self it tried to shape me

toward. As if that let me
off the other hooks.

PLASTIC: A PERSONAL HISTORY

How can I find a way to praise
it? Do the early inventors and embracers
churn with regret? I don't think my parents
—born in the swing toward ubiquity—chew
and chew and chew on plastic. But of course they
do. Bits in water, food-flesh, air.
And their parents? I remember Dad
mocking his mother's drawer of saved
rubber bands and his father-in-law's red,
corroded jerry can, patched and patched,
never replaced for new, for never-
rusting.
       Cash or plastic? Plastic. Even
for gum. We hate the $5 minimum.
Bills paperless, automatic, almost
unreal.
       My toys were plastic, castle
and circus train and yo-yo. Did my lunches
ever get wrapped in waxed paper or
was it all Saran, Saran, Saran?
                1950-something,
Sarah's mom was given, in Girl Scouts, a navy sheet
of plastic to cut, sew, and trim with white piping
into pouches for camping. Sarah has it still,
brittle but useful. Merit badge for waterproofing.
For everlasting.
        You, too, must have heard stories,
now quaint as carriages, of first plastic, pre-plastic.
Eras of glass, waxed cloth, and tin.
Of shared syringes.

All our grocery bags, growing up,
were paper. Bottom hefted on forearm, top
crunched into grab. We used them

to line the kitchen garbage pail.

                         Not that long
ago, maybe fifteen years, I made purses for my sisters
out of putty-colored, red-lettered plastic Safeway
bags. I'd snag a stack each time I went, then fold
and sew, quilt with bright thread, line with thrift store
blouses. They were sturdy and beautiful. Rainproof
and light. Clever. So clever.

                         I regret them.
And the plastic toothpicks, folders, shoes that seemed
so cheap, so easy, so use-again and thus
less wasteful, then. What did we do before
to-go lids? Things must have just spilled
and spilled.

          Do you know
what I mean? I mean, what pearl forms
around a grain of plastic in an oyster?
Is it as beautiful? Would you wear it?
Would you buy it for your daughter
so she in turn could pass it down and
pass it down and pass it down?

AT THE MÜTTER MUSEUM

Philadelphia, 2023

my favorite exhibit is not
the goiters or the soap lady,
her body encased in wax
her own body made, not
the skull collection or
the floral arrangements
of human hair, but
the library,
                which creaks
with information, walnut walls
of card catalogues, hundreds
of bronze tongues waiting
for my finger's pull,
                      notecards
indexing all worth knowing up
to 1938 about the body. Which,
when I searched, included
                         homeostasis
and hookworm, meningitis and
menstruation, but not
homosexuality, not
menopause.

～～～

. . . I figured what it was, but,
really, what I care was that there
was something I should (or should not)

have understood sounding all around
us, a thrum of deep time, of dream across
strange distances. I listen still.

BELL

Lucky when my shift on deck aligned with early
light and I could polish the bell: waist
and shoulder, head and lip.
                              I'd toggle open
the gear locker, grab the tin of Nevr-Dull stuffed
with redolent wadding, rip off a chunk and begin
to rub away the night's tarnish.

                              That summer
I also came to know the burnishment of met desire,
of a body's shine against another body like first
light glinting on polished brass.
                              Once, softly,
I tugged the bell's forbidden pull,
                              touched

                    clapper

            to mouth.

            Long-waiting sound rang
                    into the hull of my ear.

FIRST LOVE

Today, adjusting my jacket
in strong wind, I look down
to the hem, remember the neat
way she'd pull up the bottom
zipper—quick, decisive—to open
a gap for her hips. Who are we,

those many years ago,
to our current selves? Twice
a decade, we meet for tea, polite
about the others we've gone on
to love. Her small hands. How

they seemed capable of almost
anything: thumb nudging
a throttle to come alongside
a dock; what we did below
decks and in the gear locker,

the smell of burned nylon
from the line cutter, a thin,
heated blade that separates
strands and cauterizes them
so they won't fray, all
around us, everything I wanted
to be, awakening.

Kiss me like a limpkin

we joked after seeing one go at
a snail. *Kiss me like a limpkin.* Meaning
really get in there and go for the meat. Or
like an avocet—chin swept across my shoulder's
skin, bill slightly parted. Don't kiss me
like a heron, quick, hard stab and retreat.
Or like a turkey (random pecks). I'd take it
like a sanderling, though, stippling the shoreline
of my thigh. And, yes,

                     yes! Like a shoveler.
Your wide, particular mouthbill, tight as a coin
purse until you seek to satisfy your hunger and then,
agape, seeking together, aswirl, we help each other get
what we want, circling to spin up what will gratify.
Kiss me like a shoveler in an ecstasy of shovelers,
all of us one big pinwheel now, a rave, water rippling
out from our twirl, from the serious business
of our mouths, free of any self-

                    consciousness,
focused on satisfaction, light gleaming on the lustrous
black-green or soft chinchilla of the backs
of our bent and intent heads.

Skiff

All summer, she sat alongside our fence.
We cleared the wasp nests from her

gunwales. We caulked and tried to seal
her soft transom. Luckily, we couldn't

see her from any of the places we liked to sit
and ease into the day or the day's end. Each gale,

we were relieved to not have her banging
at the dingy dock. Each calm dawn, a spark

of plans to get her launched that, each time, failed
(the borrowed hitch, the illegal trailer's plates, malaise). We

had a name for her, *Noctiluca*, bright sparks that, lucky
nights, flare water at any stirring. Was it a failure?

Circumstance? *Skiff.* From the old High German
skif, which evolved to *ship* and grew masts,

bowsprits. We'd scraped the barnacles, painted
her hull. She was ready. She didn't mind, I think,

the winter weather she sat through. She was more
than satellite to a larger hull. She was everything. Waiting

and unlaunched. She. We failed more
than her, that year.

Outer Space or Deep Ocean

Your heart's smaller after you've lived
in outer space, I've read. Not much
to push against.

Does it swell back, re-
plump when it returns to earth's
demanded lug like any muscle? I have

been spaced out lately,
adrift from life's usual gravities,
planktonic in the cloud, the ether,

alone (with you) in the managed
air of our rooms. *Outer
space or deep ocean?*

One friend's second
favorite icebreaker. Deep ocean.
Deep deep ocean for me

since I was a little girl. I bet
after time down there
your heart's bigger. A heavyweight

pumping against so much
pressure. But up there,
down there, do you hear

your heart more, or less? Alone,
I hear mine (more or less). Or
I feel it, beating in what holds it.

My body. Erratic. Normal.

SWADDLED, NO MATTER

for Gracie

Easier to think of the quilt
buried with her, wrapped
around her deep-ish in the yard's
sand. Fake quilt. Pieces machine
printed on a cotton-poly bolt,
inner stuffing pulled from some chain
of polymers. It warmed us from our start
on your attic bedroom futon. That was before
her.
       The bed's bottom sheet
was a dark pine and now the same green
rings the cleared space around our house
where pear tree and ever-failing rhubarb, where
hammock and her grave.
                   It was as kind
as we could make it. I held her body, carried
those last weeks up stairs and into cars
so she could smell dune and sea. The vet
fed her treat after treat and she ate them
too fast to taste, as always. Her bowels relaxed,
the smell thick on my lap the ride back home. Better
scent than whatever sat, unmoving, in her blood.
We dug the hole. We drank Manhattans,
leaning on the shovel. The quilt, which
I'd decided
           was too worn for us,
had become hers years ago. Thin
sateen piping ran along its edge, rose
gold. Years before we met, you'd used it
in your first apartment. I've seen the photos. And
I'm not sure whether it comforts me that under
the sweetfern we planted and the slate stone

66

set on top so coyotes couldn't dig,
the quilt may still, six years on,

                                    be whole,

undegradable. It holds her bones. Her
gnawed and sleep-curled form. Her.
Gone within its unnatural persistence.

Lesson VIII: Map of North America

—redacted from Smith's Quarto, or Second Book in Geography, *1848*

     division

     division

          general divisions

Where is

          Where is Cape Farewell?

IMAGO

Shrill green cracked from the dull,
brown husk. What emerged was wet,
furled. We hunkered by the split log

the dragonfly nymph had crawled to
from the pond. Back home, our friend
was shrinking, had been

for years, disease taking strength first
from her hand, which cramped
to a tiny scrawl, then her legs, her neck

canted right, her voice rasped
to dull. We could only watch the process
for so long, the wings opening, lengthening

slowly, abdomen flopped down on bark
like a wet sock. She had to wear a cross-chest belt
to keep her in the wheelchair. It was padded

with sheepskin. She couldn't move
the Scrabble tiles, but glinted at her wins. We
set up phones on time lapse, ringed

the green darner and walked away
for an hour during which our friend's breath
was wet, her throat muscles unable

to time swallow and sigh. She
looked up less and less. When
we came back, both were gone.

Highland Light

They've wrapped the light whose beam
sweeps heath and pine and my bed
when it's not flung seaward. Don't

worry, a gap lets light escape
for those who (understandably,
justifiably) worry. At the tower's foot,

a cyclone-fence closet, unlatched,
for sensitive, outdated gear. My favorite: the
SOUND POWERED TELEPHONE

with MAGNETO HOWLER CALL.
No. I don't know what it sounds like.
I was afraid to touch it, to shout or dial. Since

1840, they've twice moved this lighthouse
back from the cliff because it's still
as necessary as it first was. Serviceberry,

first of all our flowering trees, named
because it flowers when the ground's thawed
enough to dig and bury the dead, sweeps

against the keeper's house. Which is
a museum now. Look: I can be strange
and useful. We can be crumbling and still

necessary. I think we can even be repaired.
There's nothing I want to bury this spring.

On Reality

I got there before even the surfers—
did you know there are still surfers?
There are. And rabbits. There are
still rabbits, though so many people
don't think to look for them. Don't even
see them scrunched on the grass, still
but for their working jaws, working
noses. The undertow was strong.

Big waves from some offshore system
even though the sky was calm. I felt
the ocean want to pull me out

and north; I stood and leaned against
it. That and the cool made me feel strong.
I felt strong again. As if I might deserve

some luck or love. There are also, still,
huge schools of pogies that, when seen
from any height, look like cloud shadows
darkening the sea. Today, someone
posted a photo I was in—the whole team
grinning as we headed to port—and I didn't

recognize the wild joy on my face. There are
still cobblers (both kinds) and jackalopes.
As much as there were ever. Proof of some
dream we keep sharing. Some strange dream
we tell someone we love about
hoping they've had it, too.

THE GUIDES GO ASHORE AHEAD

One of us scrambles up a slope
and pretends not to notice
the gyrfalcon's protest.

One goes back for a forgotten hat,
which pisses off the sailor
who has to make

an extra shuttle. Two kick
at tideline gravel, flirting, scouting
for a better landing site.

One lies down and pretends to be alone.

One scans for bears, plots a route,
scouts for things to exclaim over,
later, with an audience.

Another pretends to do the same, but
looks for hare, imagines hunt.
One fiddles with the first aid kit,

one ignores the radio call, one
pockets a fossil, photographs
the place devoid of people.

One looks up to see the full boats
coming. Then we gather at the shore,
no longer individual.

TAKING A FIX

is not the same as getting one. No smack
or horse, though there may be mares'
tails. Fixed, for the dog, was

not her choice. Ours. Once, I told
myself that the key to a happy life
was to fix one thing daily—broken

lamp, loud hinge—believing that
small accomplishments could ease
the wallow of bigger failings. To fix,

in chemistry, is to stop something's
evolution: body to dirt, germ to disease,
light to photographic darkness in fixer.

I learned to *take a fix* at sea where, each
hour, we pencil the chart with an X,
the compass heading, and the time.

We check what's outside against
the drawn shores, depth-
sounder against inked fathoms,

note buoys and lights marking spots
proven dangerous. Here. And
here. And here. Thus, the way

we've arrived where we think
we are at this moment.

April, Provincetown

We're down on the dock studded
with clamshells gulls have dropped
to break open on the floats. Low tide. The first

thing I see in the clear, spring water
is a condom. Then, scribed by telsons
and fringed by delicate claws,

the scooched trails of horseshoe crabs
coming to lay eggs in sand. I'd like
one year to see the hatched young scuttle

out. A guy on the float pokes down
with a gaff, pulls up a lawn chair and puts it,
tenderly, on the dock. We've been looking

at double-crested cormorants building
their nests. All spring, they fly in
with fucus, grass-root, rope, jock

strap bands. Their mouths are azure
with lust. It was so beautiful
to be there with you.

Identification

Our faces, my sweet, are no longer blank
slates, remade each day. At rest, they speak.

We know the whales most easily
by their scars. Coral's fluke tooth-raked,
Piano's flank sliced by prop into keys.

What's wrong? you ask, & I'm pleased
you notice what I thought I'd hid.

Pele's barnacle dot. Music, Pleats, Venom,
Cajun, all marked by killer whale, by boat, by
what rope & line have rubbed raw.

Nothing, I say, noting the darker spot
on your cheek that's emerged the last few years.

I focus the lens. Document the known &
the new. Pink means fresh wound,
the body healing.

I'm less interested in those old marks
than what worries begin to persist now.

I note it all: time, location, behavior. Is there
a calf? Yes, six months old & already twice
scarred, twice cut free. Maybe that wound will heal.

I hook a bra, pull on shorts, glad for what they hide.
I know my hidden stories. Stretchmarks, sag, scar.

Naked, unhoused, every surface surrounded
by moving matter—how can we know a whale?
Sound thrumming up the jaw to ear

What (not what, but how, with which tone) *did
you say?* What presses, unsaid, behind it?

voiced inside the body's dark resonances. Where echoes
can't be known, can be ignored, can offer
what we all turn away from.

BUILDING A GREENLAND KAYAK

It's fine if you don't comb the long shore
for a piece of wood from the treed land south.
Fine if you go to Home Depot with a list.
                    If cash, not time, purchases
the raw materials.
                        Not even your own life
will fit you as well as this boat. And your own life

can't bend and flex like this lashed frame, wood
and sinew shifting, fifty pieces of rib, gunwhale, keelson
held by pegs and string.
                        Start with the span
of your arms. Three times: its length. Beam:
your hips plus a fist.
                        How do you measure
a task? Know your body will meet it,
enspirit not shirk? Focus your misfit self
on the story pole:
                    set an eight foot board
on a scrap of 2x2. Seat yourself, legs out, and shift
until it stops teetering then mark the set of your heels, tent
of your knees, spot where your weight comes down. This boat
is your body.
                If it pulls in a sea, rebuild it. If the bow
catches air in a wind, build again.

In Lyme Country

I could allow myself
to lie down in the new
grasses, the soon-to-bloom
starflowers—but only
if I were willing, later,
to look at every inch
of my body. Only if you
would slowly comb
through my hair and
along the parts of me
I find hard to examine.
Looking, with love,
for danger.

PERMEABLE

after Leah Wong

Below us: water (fresh lens). And
below that: a different water
(salt soused). This youngest end
of a glacier-spat spit,
this outwash plain,
grains permeable, percolating,

angular, rough, tilted
piled & drifted into
dunes, swales. Space
between the planes. Slip & seep.

How does it hold? How are
we held? As we bustle, as we duck
whatever current licks
at us. A comfort to river

my own salt through a pond
which is an open eye of the water
body (aquifer) a well sucks
from under backyard sand
(pull too deep & you'll
draw salt). We float, placid,

though not untouched by what falls,
heavy, from seeming-clear sky into
nymph-body, fish-body. Or what
fins up from salt-depth, toothed. Or
riptides (diver lost this summer
& the body held two days
before washed ashore). Sorrow,

I have felt you, seeping
　　　　　as the pond's larger body seeps,
　　flows slow, finally rivers out
a few feet below mean high into larger
　　　　　water—you've seen those small rivers,
underworld-cool, vein-like & branching
　　　　into our porous, hazardous world.

Today, Alongside a Fresh-dead Humpback Whale

Flitter over water over
fat-slick, gobbets plucked,
the dark souls of storm petrels,
restless and hungry and
pattering.
Up-slick,
the body, now carcass and source,
belly up. This whale I watched
last summer as calf, nursing
from his half-fluked mother
(Venom) who had survived
something borne before
I met her.
And now:

Ripple then fin then shark.
A great white rides up
the throat-slope—blubber
wobbled, grabbed, torn. Water
now blooded. Another
shadow-glow circles, feeds. Another.

Nodal point at this moment in all the gulf's
waters, you gather us. We flock. The sea
calms downtide from your flank, oiled
smooth by what you slough. And,
stink thick and coating, we take
you in. We watch, breathe,
now part of your new,
dissembled ongoing.

"Memory Rowing the Passage of Time"

is what I'd title this sculpture, if asked. And
this is what my new mind, which is an older
mind, feels like: an oar with the blade
so thoroughly drilled it's more hole

than wood. I'm reading about different
cultures of time—linear (the past
behind you), visible (future
at your back), vertical (time falling,

your body an hourglass), coiled
(loops touching again and again).
Janice has covered the oar in something
like moleskin, which was never

the skin of a tiny, shy mammal, but heavy
cotton roughed to softness. I like hacks
for anticipated wear. One spring, I sewed
leather cuffs onto our skiff's oars, pushed

waxed twine through punches with a sailpalm,
which made me ridiculously enamored
of myself, sitting in the sunlit drive, thinking
if only someone could come by and see this, they'd

have to fall in love with me. Janice's oar hangs,
vertical, braced by a special-made mount. If
it dropped, it would break, but my heart's not
in my throat. One version of time

is a circle, Ouroboros, the world's waters
held inside, everything inside, held. Each day,
there are little moments I can't reach back
and touch, which makes it easier to pull
the oar. Which makes it harder to get anywhere.

Appendix: To Draw a Map of the World

redacted from Smith's Quarto, or Second Book in Geography, *1848*

I.

open the dividers
the dividers will describe the opposite
open the dividers still farther,

. The true extent
of the dividers will be found by trial.

Continue this   , until you have drawn all the parallels.
and describe the opposite   .

II.

To draw a map of North America

Assume
a distance   . Set off
a little space beyond the limits

until you have passed   through

the point

Take a flexible ruler   bend
and curve it   .
careful to keep

difference
delineated   .

Dispatch from this Summer

Lymantria dispar dispar

Frayed, moth-eaten, vulnerable. Those Florida dancers
gunned down & my young self coming out dancing & pathetic
fallacy (*dispar dispar*) crawls all over June's fresh oaks,

gnawing them to a February canopy. The news, bad
oracle, gnaws fact & rumor. Above, unrelenting
mastication, defoliation. *Lymantria*, 'destroyer,' all else gone,

you hump up even the stiff needles of pines. What will happen
come winter, no sun stored? Should we spray? Should
we shun social media? Avoid large aggregations? How

hot the birds must be, now unshaded in their nests. (Guilty
thrill of peering down on black-billed cuckoos calling.)
Other wings. The white towering of Kushner's angels

sentry for Orlando's mourning. We consider what it would take
to pick the trees clean. Could we? The bark the grass the ground
writhes. In a grove in China, a grim documentary:

honeybees gone, people pollinate fruit trees by hand. I twitch away
from one caterpillar dangling from its thread, hanging by
the silk that brought it here, to the New World, to Massachusetts

even, because some merchant in 1869—while Grant
took the presidency & Elizabeth Cady Stanton spoke
before Congress & the Golden Spike was hammered

into Utah & the South fumbled through what's called
Reconstruction—thought *crop, harvest, riches* & hoped
the long, expensive trek to mulberry unnecessary. We gnaw

through news feeds. We post & share, unsure
if we are offering or consuming. In the forest, a constant
heavy frass. On my side of the river, healthy trees. Oak leaves

thick & dark. In the dance clubs near me, there is
dancing. But introduction, dispersal . . . In the week
after Pulse, in Massachusetts, 450% more guns like that gun

were sold. If you can stand to walk a narrow path through the leafless
forest, you can arrive at a circle of water that will allow your body
to be beautifully held, whoever you are. It's true, you'll have to return

by the same path, go back through those apocalyptic trees. If
I had waited a month to begin this poem, I would have begun
with the re-leafing. Fuzzed red growth in late July, white moth-

flutter among the trunks not angelic, but like paper corners
that escaped arson or accident. And, plastered to bark,
the russet humps of eggs I scrape with a stick—vengeful,

hopeful, despairing—even as they are being laid.

      —North Truro, 2016

HELD/TREASURED/SECRET

To carry something fragile—a vole
skull, for example, or the thin,
ridged shell of a paper nautilus—make
a cage of yourself, curl fingers stiff
around a space you could close

to a fist. And at first it's easy. But you fear
your scattered mind: *Careful care*
ful careful each footfall. You worry
about the little gap where your
smallest finger touches

your healthline. The short walk home
stretches long. Try a few positions
of the arm—held ahead, elbow dug
into waist, palm cupped up; ulna tight
across diaphragm or ovary; radius

tucked below the hip's wing. It's not
easy, though nothing is heavy. Your hand
sweats and cramps and one part of you longs
to just let it go. But you picked it up. You've
carried it this far. And now it must be held

until you find a safe place
—desk, car dash, sill by the door—
to put it down.

WHEN ONE KNOWN TO YOU DIES,
THE REARRANGING OF SPACE AND TIME BEGINS

for Ladders, 2019 (Balaenoptera physalus)

A rib (I know whose) in
the harbor under
waves. How

heavy would it be, hefted? Low
tide will bare it,
will allow

pickers to take it, make
it décor—whale bone
with tulips, leaching

minerals, oil, the perennials
stronger for it. Up
the beach

the rest of him. Un-
scattered and held still
by sinew, flesh.

Spine and ribs but no longer
the jaw, which when he first
washed up ashore

and was flayed by flensers and sun,
proved to be broken.
We knew him,

this fin whale, Ladders. I can't remember
the year, the moment of
my first

sighting or resighting of his stuttered
prop scar, long healed, an easy
marker. Who

was I then? Young and newly
arrived, sorrows vast, and
losses, it must

be said, negligible. Negligible.
What does his rib curve
now? That

space filled by water. That
emptiness. And knowledge
of what it once held.

BINNACLE

cylindrical non-ferrous container for magnetic compass

It stands at the gut because
that's where we feel the pull
of a course. Right or wrong.
It was so hard to steer true
at first, hands slick on the wheel,
straining to avoid disaster
in the drift between 345 and
330.
         Numbers slide port
and starboard of the lubber line
as I try to *catch the compass*. We spin
around the card that never moves.
We correct for standard deviation,
the ship's own pull.
               I'm often sure
I'm running true, but once, out
in fog, I thought I could steer my way
back to the ship without a compass.
We drove & drove &
            finally I
radioed the bridge to sound the horn.
It sounded, distant, from nowhere
I expected.
         As for local deviations,
don't worry, corrections are listed
on the chart.
           In the pilot house,
I rest my chin on the binnacle's cool brass
dome. It's lovely and it tells me nothing
of how I'll get it wrong from here.

UNDER THE GREAT WAVE

Hokusai: Inspiration and Influence, *Seattle Art Museum, 2023*

We walk through rooms of what it foams up
from, what foams up after, what flows back to
communal sea. Frame after frame framing
that familiar crest—his wave in Lego, in
graffiti. Also his Fuji and Fuji and Fuji
                                film sold
in green boxes, back when we were still manual. You
preferred it to Kodak's warmth. Its saturated cool
clear even in murky weather, better
for sea-light's blues.
                     We've never seen the same colors,
a subject of our sweetest fights these many years:
my eyes, your shirt, a scaup's neck.
                         I once read
some people, women mostly, have an extra
cone that shifts their spectrum's span. You
once met a colorblind tracker who spotted more
cougar, more bighorn because he couldn't see
what blended them. When I pay attention I can
be a good spotter. Motion.
                   Difference. Maybe
a skill developed young, in Seattle, looking at her
and her and her to see who might be what. Or him
and him to see what danger. *I trust your eyes*, you've
said. More than once. I still thrill to it, but lately your
eyes seem sharpest for my flaws, which are in no way
adorable or amusing
               scary as a breaker
about to crash on a boat off Kanagawa, Fuji
in the background. Hokusai's original
print is small enough to fit into a file folder,
is tucked around one little wall across

from the German printmaker's
                              huge tribute.
To make it, she knelt with a chisel on a sheet
of plywood, carved warbled lines that, inked
and pressed onto spume-white paper, the eye blurs
to completion, floods to fill as *wave.*
                              Like
old newsprint shots of war or protest, grained
and legible,
              like the papers under our bed
in flat files of your Act-Up, your Dyke March, your
No Nukes pics in the Boston alts before we met, before
your lens turned to polar bear, walrus, eider.
Those images stored in slides that show
the past when light passes
through them
                  as light, greened, passes through a wave
at its height before it breaks, showing the bodies inside
who we hope know how to play with huge
energy
          that has pummeled me
and of course will fade to calm,
away, eventually.

ALL WITHOUT INCIDENT

Last week, asleep, I rose
from our attic bed of this,
our fourth shared home,
walked down the steep, illegal
stairs, opened the back door
& stepped outside. *It's nice
here,* I said, *we should stay
a few days longer,* I said.

Or so you say I said.

~~~~~

A thrum of deep time, of dream across
strange distances. I listen still.

NOTES

"Considering the Hadal Zone:" Also known as the hadopelagic zone, the hadal zone ranges between 3.7 to 6.8 miles below the ocean's surface within the narrow, v-shaped oceanic trenches of our earth's deepest depths. The Provincetown AIDS memorial is designed by sculptor Lauren Ewing and was dedicated on June 1, 2018. On June 18, 2023, *Titan*, a submersible operated by OceanGate as a tourism venture, imploded while descending to visit the *Titanic*. Five people, two who worked for OceanGate and three tourists, including a father and son, were aboard.

"Shadow (*Charcharodon carcharias*):" Elasmobranchs (sharks, skates, and rays) have sensitive organs, the ampullae of Lorenzini, that allow them to detect electrical fields and pulses (like heartbeats) in the water. They also, like most fish, have a "lateral line" that allows them to sense movement, vibration, and shifts in pressure around them. The tags I refer to are various satellite and acoustic "pinger" tags placed on sharks by scientists.

"Origin Story, Re-wrought:" The "dog watch" is typically a shorter, two-hour work shift (most nautical watches are four hours). Dog watches are used to rotate sailors through various working shifts, meaning the bad and good are equally enjoyed.

"Silver Hake:" It's illegal to keep fish or other catch that were not the intended target of a fishing voyage. This "bycatch" has to be tossed back. The aim is to encourage fishers to be specific and precise in their efforts and to disallow "oopsies" landings of illegal but valuable catch. However, much of the tossed-back bycatch does not survive the trauma of being caught.

"Lesson III: The Divisions, Illustrated:" This poem (and others in the sequence) are taken from *Smith's Quarto, or Second Book in Geography*, 1848, an early textbook in US schools. Spacings represent, roughly, the distance between "saved" words.

"Touchy:" "Touch me" is from Stanley Kunitz's beautiful poem by the same name.

"Spinnaker:" Healthy whale bones are 60% fat, and the oil they hold seeps out over decades, turning the first-white bones brown. The vomer bone in a whale runs from the nostrils/blowholes out along the top of the skull to the front of the upper jaw. Whale flukes (the tail) are made of connective tissue/cartilage, thus are not preserved after life as bones are.

"Intergenerational:" True story.

"Notes on the Wharf:" Eva Silva, Mary Jason, Bea Cabral, Frances Raymond, and Almeda Segura are the names of local women whose 10' x 14' portraits are featured in "They Also Faced the Sea," an installation by Norma Holt and Ewa Nogiec (2003). In 2013, the United States vs. Windsor Supreme Court decision rendered DOMA (the Defense of Marriage Act) unconstitutional, thus federally recognizing same-sex marriage throughout the United States.

"At the Smallpox Cemetery, Provincetown:" The quoted lines are from CD Wright's posthumously published book about beech trees (and, of course, so much more), *Casting Deep Shade: An Amble* (2019). Pages 50, 9, 69, 198, respectively.

"Ded Reckoning:" *Encyclopedia Brown,* anyone?

"From Sea, Toward Sea:" Rachel Carson, in *Under the Sea-Wind* (1941), wrote about the life of the American eel (*Anguilla rostrata)* and brought their fascinating life history to the page for a general reader for the first time. Eel larvae, partly blind and translucent, are described by many as resembling willow leaves. "Sweet water" is another way to describe fresh water (vs. salt).

"At the Mütter Museum:" Described as "America's finest museum of medical history," the Mütter is a fascinating and sometimes grotesque experience of specimens and instruments displayed in 19th-century glass-case style. It first opened in 1863.

"Imago:" In biology, the imago, also called the imaginal state, is the last stage of an insect's metamorphosis, the stage of maturity. It is also, in psychology, the unconscious image of one dearly loved.

"In Lyme Country:" This poem refers to the dangers of deer ticks and the Lyme disease they can potentially carry (as well as other debilitating diseases).

"Today, Alongside a Fresh-dead Humpback Whale:" Storm petrels, some sailors believe, are the embodiment of those lost at sea.

"Memory Rowing the Passage of Time:" A sculpture by Janice Redman, *Feathering* (2021, wool and wood, 60" x 5"), inspired this poem. *Feathering* is featured in the cover image of *SOFAR*.

"Dispatch from this Summer:" This poem is in response to the 2016 Pulse nightclub shooting in Orlando, Florida. *Lymantria dispar dispar* is the Latin name for the spongy moth (formerly the gypsy moth). Because of anticipated disruption by anti-queer factions at the services for those slain, people flew down and wore the costumes from Tony Kushner's award-winning play about AIDS, *Angels in America*, to stand in solidarity and protect the mourners. Frass is the term for insect poop.

"Under the Great Wave:" The German printmaker is Christiane Baumgartner (1967–), and the poem describes her print "The Wave," 2017, 149.3 x 210.4 cm. Woodcut on Kozo paper. Edition of six.

ACKNOWLEDGMENTS

The poems below have been published in journals and anthologies, sometimes in different versions. I am so grateful to the support of the editors for this work while it was in process—and for their advocacy of new literature in the world.

About Place: "Fulcrum," "Held/Treasured/Secret," "Identification," "Dispatch from this Summer," "Silver Hake"

Academy of American Poets Poem-A-Day: "Learning to Swim"

Alaska Quarterly Review: "Allegiance," "Erratic," "The California Coast"

Appalachia: "Articulation"

Atlantic Monthly: "Touchy"

Campfire Stories: Cape Cod: "Shadow (*Carcharodon carcharias*)"

Cape Cod Review: "At the Mütter Museum," "Chock," "Remember the way"

Copper Nickel: "At fifty, I discover vagility"

Elementals: "Learning to Swim"

The Eloquent Poem: "Lesson III: The Divisions, Illustrated"

Green Humanities: "Drone"

Kenyon Review: "Permeable," "When One Known to you Dies, the Rearranging of Space and Time Begins"

Kinship: Belonging in a World of Relations: "When One Known to you Dies, the Rearranging of Space and Time Begins," "Dispatch from this Summer"

Leon Literary Review: "First Love"

A Literary Field Guide to Northern Appalachia: "From Sea, Toward Sea"

New Orleans Review: "Building a Greenland Kayak"

Orion: "Imago"

Our Provincetown: Intimate Portraits: "Notes on the Wharf"

Phaitude: "The Guides Go Ashore Ahead"

Ploughshares: "At the Smallpox Cemetery, Provincetown"

Plume: "Sissy-Fists"

Plume Poetry 10: "Today, Alongside a Fresh-dead Humpback Whale"

Poetry: "Plastic: A Personal History"

Poetry Northwest: "Origin Story, Re-Wrought"

Quarterly West: "Swaddled, No Matter"

Reading Queer: Poetry in a Time of Chaos: "Dispatch from this Summer"

Rewilding: Poems for the Environment: "Permeable"

Sensing: Attending to the Wonder and Vitality of Nature: "Spinnaker"

The Sun: "Plastic: A Personal History"

Terrain.org: "A Mouth Like a Sailor," "Bell," "The Paper Wasps"

Tin House: "Lesson VIII: Map of North America"

Thank you to my writer-family who read poems, offered advice, and helped share this journey: Christine Byl, Gabriel Fried, CMarie Fuhrman, Sean Hill, Donika Kelly, Anne Haven McDonnell, Jill McDonough, John Nieves, Miller Oberman, Janice Redman, Derek Sheffield, Alexandra Teague, and so many more. Also my boat-family, whale-family, chosen family, and blood-family.

Thank you Ragdale Foundation, TS Eliot House, and Peaked Hill Trust for time out of time to dream and delve during residencies.

Lisa, still, you.